AFTER
THE
DINOSAURS

The names of early mammals
may be hard to say,
but finding out about them
is fun for us today.

A FIRST TIME READER™

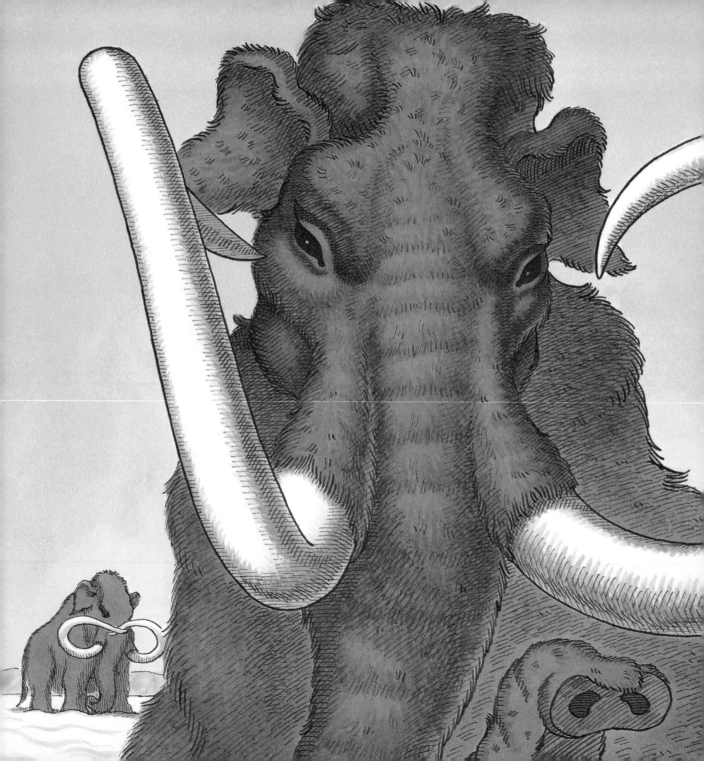

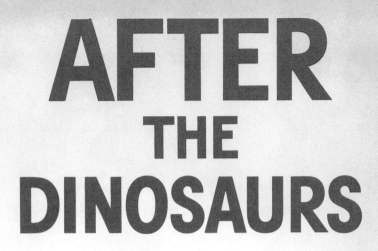

AFTER THE DINOSAURS

By Stan & Jan Berenstain
Illustrated by
Michael Berenstain

Random House 🏠 New York

Copyright © 1988 by Berenstains, Inc. All rights reserved under International and Pan-American Copyright Conventions. Published in the United States by Random House, Inc., New York, and simultaneously in Canada by Random House of Canada Limited, Toronto.

Library of Congress Cataloging-in-Publication Data:
Berenstain, Stan. After the dinosaurs. (A first time reader) SUMMARY: Rhyming text and illustrations present a broad range of prehistoric mammals, from the ratlike triconodon to the spectacular woolly mammoth. 1. Mammals, Fossil—Juvenile literature. [1. Mammals, Fossil. 2. Prehistoric animals] I. Berenstain, Jan. II. Berenstain, Michael, ill. III. Title. IV. Series: Berenstain, Stan. First time reader. QE881.B52 1988 569 88-42588 ISBN: 0-394-80518-6 (pbk.); 0-394-90518-0 (lib. bdg.)

Manufactured in the United States of America   1 2 3 4 5 6 7 8 9 0

When we speak of dinosaurs,
it seems fair to say
that even though they are extinct
we see them more each day.

They are popular in books,
on shirts, in kits, as toys.
They are the favorite creatures
of many girls and boys.

But there were stranger kinds
of prehistoric beast.
They evolved on earth
after dinosaurs had ceased.

These creatures were the mammals
of prehistoric days.
They were different from the dinosaurs
in some important ways.

Mammals are warm-blooded.
Their skin has fur or hair.
They have their babies live
in some sort of lair.

It is very likely
that Triconodon was small.
It was an early mammal—
perhaps the earliest of all.

Tri-CON-o-don

It is thought to have been ratlike.
But scientists confess
that how this creature looked
is but an educated guess.

The mammal
we call horse today
goes back in time
a long, long way—
fifty million years,
in fact.
In the early horse's case,
we can be exact.

Eohippus
(Fifty million years ago)

E-o-HIP-pus

Orohippus
(Forty million years ago)

Or-o-HIP-pus

Mesohippus
(Thirty million years ago)

Mes-o-HIP-pus

Merychippus
(Ten million years ago)

Mer-yc-HIP-pus

They were very horselike,
with graceful bodies, horselike tails,
and hooflike toes for running,
instead of claws or nails.

But they were very different
in one important way.
They were small compared to
the horse we know today.

Yes, horses were small
way back when.
Certain birds, however,
were much, much bigger then.

Diatryma, for example,
of which few of us have heard,
was, to put it mildly,
a very big, big bird.

Prehistoric mammals,
which then were small and weak,
had to keep an eye out
for its giant beak.

Di-a-TRY-ma

Another early bird,
scientists confirm,
was Phororhacus, who
caught much more than the worm.

Pho-ROR-ha-cus

But the world was changing,
and it wasn't very long
(just twenty million years)
till prehistoric mammals
grew quite big and strong.

Though it had no trunk or tusks
and was rather like a pig,
Moeritherium was
the start of something big.

It was the earliest elephant
and, so to speak, gave birth
to the mightiest line of mammals
that ever roamed the earth.

Moe-ri-THER-i-um

A very early elephant
was Gomphotherium.
It was an early warning
of much bigger things to come.

Gom-pho-THER-i-um

Platybelodon
was the strangest of the group.
What should have been its trunk
was, instead, a scoop—
with big, flat teeth for sifting
river mud and goop.

Plat-y-BEL-o-don

Deinotherium had mighty tusks.
Of that there is no doubt.
But why it grew them upside down
is hard to figure out.

Dein-o-THER-i-um

The mighty Mastodon
had super-duper strength.
Its fossil tusks have measured
seven feet in length.

MAS-to-don

The famous Woolly Mammoth
is a very special case.
Though this creature is extinct,
we have more than just a trace:

Some explorers, digging in
against the Arctic's icy breeze,
found one frozen whole
in Mother Earth's deep freeze.

WOOL-ly MAM-moth

Indricotherium,
the beast of Baluchistan,
was the biggest land-bound mammal
since the earth began.

In-dri-co-THER-i-um

Elasmotherium

E-las-mo-THER-i-um

Though except for fossil bones
these mammals are no more—
they are the ancestors of
modern animals galore.

Smilodon

SMIL-o-don

Megatherium

Meg-a-THER-i-um

Rhinos, tigers, sloths, and camels are all descended from prehistoric mammals.

Procamelus

Pro-CAM-e-lus

Perhaps the most important mammal
since the world began
was a prehistoric mammal
known as Early Man.

So very much has happened
since humankind began,
whether *we* become extinct
is up to modern man.